ENVIRONMENTAL SYST

Temperate Grasslands

D. C. Money

Evans

Evans Brothers Limited

Published by Evans Brothers Limited
Montague House, Russell Square, London WC1B 5BX

Evans Brothers (Nigerian Publishers) Limited
PMB 5164, Jericho Road, Ibadan

First published 1982

Acknowledgements
Canada House, pp. 31, 37, 43
The Lockwood Survey Corporation, p. 44
The Mansell Collection, p. 26
Novosti Press Agency, pp. 12, 20, 33, 39
John Topham Picture Library, p. 27
US Dept. of Agriculture, Soil Conservation Service, pp. 30, 45 (above)
US Dept. of Interior, Water and Power Resources Service, p. 45 (below)
US Travel Service, front cover

Line illustrations by Reproduction Drawings

Filmset and printed in Great Britain by
BAS Printers Limited, Over Wallop, Hampshire

ISBN 0 237 29270 X PRA 7297

Contents

Cover photograph Most of the world's temperate grasslands have become more intensive systems of energy conversion—with the help of huge inputs by man. Here the pattern of alternate strips of wheat and fallow reflect a scientific approach and the use of mechanical energy to make the best use of the dry grasslands of Montana.

A Systems Approach

The definition and examination of systems, more or less simplified for study purposes, enables the complexities of the real, observed world to be considered in an orderly manner. We can see more clearly the interrelationships between the components of a system and the flows of energy and matter which take place within it. We simplify to see how the system is structured and to consider how the components may be further studied and measured. Simplifications involve subjective actions. It is important to define the limits of study and to specify the systems and sub-systems under consideration. In practice, field measurements and analysis are required to establish causal relationships between vegetation forms and the environmental variables selected for study.

Here we are concerned with ecosystems and human socio-economic systems and their interactions. Matter and energy continuously pass through a mature ecosystem; but within it the complex plant and animal organisms and the elements of their habitat are approximately in a state of equilibrium. In examining the world's temperate grasslands we are faced with the fact that because of their gentle relief, fertile soils, and abundant natural grasses and forbs there has been large-scale exploitation for grazing and grain production, with a consequent disturbance of the vegetation/soil balance over huge areas. As these grasslands extend through many degrees of latitude, the composition of the vegetation varies considerably, especially near their margins. However, the absence of major relief barriers and the effects of continentality have made for gradual changes in climatic and soil conditions and in the vegetation. A systems approach enables us to study selected areas by isolating relevant variables in the lithosphere, atmosphere and biosphere, and considering in turn their individual influences and their combined effects. This also enables us to assess more clearly the changes brought about by economic development, and the possible consequences of future development.

It is probable that the characteristics of the grasslands have long been modified by the attentions of wild herbivores. Now that the vegetation has been drastically affected by human interference, there is a tendency to regard the improved pastures, crops and woodland plantings as no longer 'natural'. But the characteristics of these huge areas of man's exploitation still depend on solar energy, atmospheric conditions and the availability of soil nutrients. Certainly men can alter micro-climatic and soil characteristics, but within these broad areas of temperate grassland elements of the atmosphere and lithosphere still exert strong controls: this is evident when technological achievements are disrupted, as has so often happened in the history of civilisation.

The Vegetation-Soil System

In any ecosystem within the broad areas shown in Fig. 4 no physical or biotic factor operates in complete independence; everything within it is related to everything else to some degree, and there are a large number of variables. Our aims are to identify the most important variables *within* the ecosystem and the extent to which particular external variables control these relationships. Here we identify a plant system and a soil system, between which are transfers of energy and materials.

EXTERNAL VARIABLES

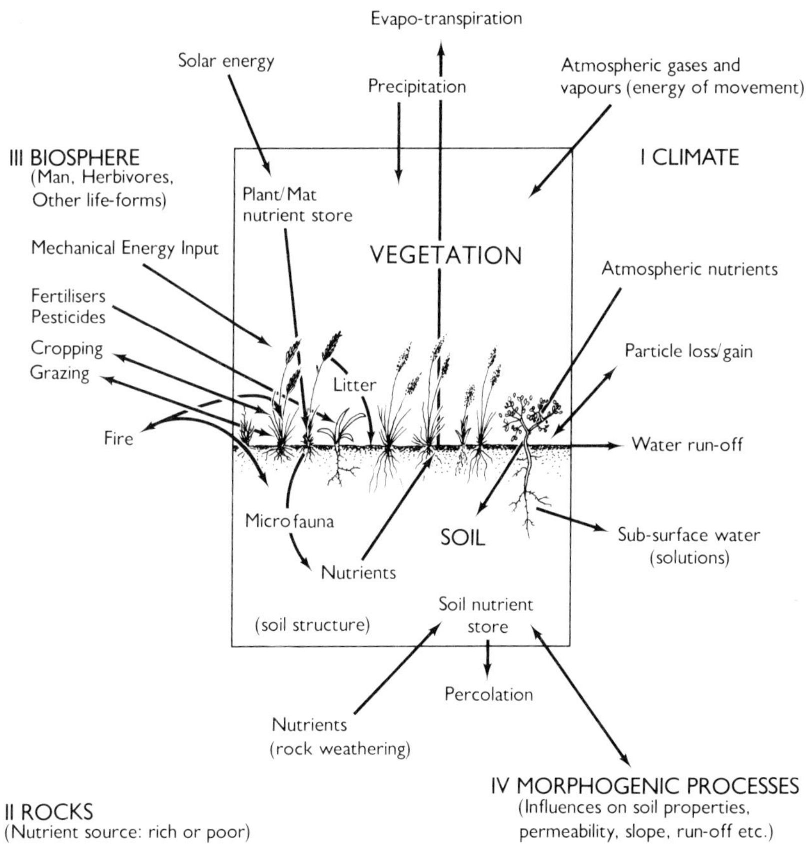

Fig. 1 These four broad categories of external variables which affect grassland soil-vegetation systems are considered separately in the book and are seen to interact in many ways.

Plant productivity largely depends on soil nutrient inputs, so we look at the interactions of those key components which affect the available nutrient store in the soil.

Fig. 1 shows an open system and the direction of exchanges of energy and matter with its environment. These are needed for its maintenance and preservation, and allow the particular grassland system to reach a state where its properties appear almost constant over a long period—approaching a steady state equilibrium.

The chosen internal components are those of the plants and soil. Climatic elements are shown among the external independent variables. But climate also affects the internal variables, such as the rate of weathering of the rocks, the release of soil nutrients, losses through leaching, and saline accumulations through persistent evaporation. Whichever locality we examine within the great expanses of grassland, local climatic conditions affect the input and output of nutrients; though the nature of the local vegetation may be influenced by other factors.

The Availability and Storage of Nutrients

The atmospheric elements carbon, hydrogen, oxygen and nitrogen make up 95 per cent of the dry weight of protoplasm in plants. Many other elements are needed by most living organisms, and these are made available for plants by the weathering of rocks and soil particles. Calcium, magnesium, potassium, sodium, phosphorus, sulphur, silicon, iron and aluminium are widely available—though a soil may lack a particular element. Weathering releases other elements which plants may require in very small amounts, but which are vital to their mature development—such as manganese, zinc, cobalt and copper.

Very soluble compounds are available for absorption by plants, but are apt to be lost from the soil by leaching. However, tiny clay particles in association with humus (as a clay–humus complex) can firmly retain vital metal ions (cations). These cations pass into the plants in exchange for hydrogen ions released from rootlets.

The nutrients released from solution are temporarily 'stored' in plants, together with the elements received from photosynthetic and nitrifying processes. They are returned to the surface as plant litter. When this decomposes it releases them into the soil. It also provides organic acids which may act on mineral particles and help to weather the bedrock.

Soil micro-organisms help the cycling of nutrients between plants and soil. Many of them act to break down plant litter, and nitrifying bacteria help to restore the nitrogen lost by leaching or other causes. Earthworms and other soil organisms mix the soil mineral particles and help to distribute organic matter within the soil.

The nutrient content of the plant–soil system, and the development of

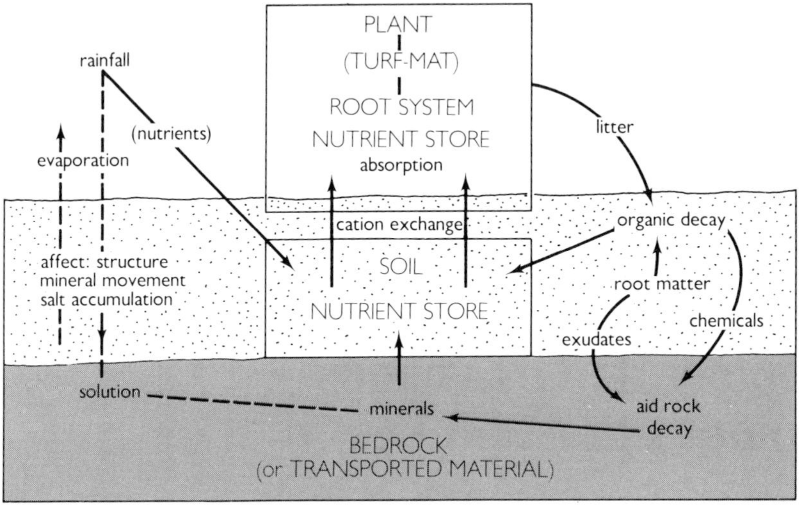

Fig. 2 The nutrient exchanges between atmosphere, soil and vegetation are simplified. In reality the interactions are complex. Nutrients derived from parent material promote plant growth; chemicals exuded by plant roots may help to liberate nutrients from mineral particles; and acids from decaying litter affect the rate of breakdown of clays. Some grassland plants release chemicals which inhibit the growth of competitive species, or even their own seedlings, and so ensure a satisfactory intake of moisture and nutrients.

the plants themselves, are affected by the rate of release of minerals from the bedrock and regolith. In fact, many of the temperate grassland soils have developed on transported material, with mixed mineral contents derived from distant sources. Particles transported by wind, water or ice have been deposited and have accumulated on plainlands. Minute dust particles transported by wind from arid areas, or from distant accumulations of dry materials, have settled to build up a loess cover of varying depth—some in eastern Asia are immensely thick. Most of the world's temperate grasslands (Fig. 4) have extensive areas of soil developed on loess. Large parts of the prairies of Canada and northern USA are mantled with glacial deposits, much of which have been redistributed by outwash. Neighbouring lands have loess derived in part from the drying glacial material. The mixture of minerals in loess, alluvium and glacial deposits provides a wide range of nutrients and forms soils of high potential fertility—though there are also gravelly outwash areas which are infertile. The nutrients in all of these parent materials, as in the more consolidated rocks, must still be made available for absorption by the plants. Moisture must be present to facilitate the chemical decomposition of the minerals which will provide the appropriate nutrients and create the solutions for plants to absorb.

It is important to realise that there are many thousand species of grass, each capable of tolerating specific ecological conditions, and that a variety of other herbaceous plants with varying tolerances make up the grassland vegetation. So that, even though certain nutrients are absent, or are denied to plants by the presence of other chemicals in the soil, there may still be a close vegetation cover made up of those grasses, sedges or forbs which can extract the particular minerals necessary for their development. We will now look at some of the characteristic associations of grassland plants.

Temperate Grasslands—Composition and Distribution

a) Composition

The grass family (Graminae) dominates these ecosystems. The structure of these herbaceous plants is illustrated in Fig. 3. In most species the blades of the leaves are nearly vertical, so that there is a high ratio of leaf surface to ground area—an efficient arrangement for productivity through photosynthesis. The grass stem increases in length from a small region at the base and just above each node. Grass thus stands up to cutting, grazing and burning better than most plants. In fact, such activities encourage growth in many grasses, for the axial buds at the base of the stem produce side shoots (tillers) whose growth is stimulated by removal of the main shoot.

Many perennial grasses have underground stems (rhizomes) with close nodes, from which new shoots emerge: bunched together, these produce a tussock form. Others have long creeping rhizomes with their nodes more widely spaced, from which new shoots and a large volume of thin, fibrous branching roots develop, forming a matted mass, or turf. The root hairs absorb water and soluble nutrients from the soil. Rapid root growth enables perennial grasses readily to colonise unvegetated surfaces.

The long, flowering stems produce seeds which, carried by the wind or attached to animals, may be widely dispersed. These may remain dormant for long periods until conditions favour germination. The grass fruit, grain, has long provided man with a direct source of food, and the plant biomass is an indirect source via herbivores and grain-fed animals.

In these ecosystems grasses dominate the herbaceous stratum (field), in association with sedges (grass-like *cyperaceae*) and many other herbs, forbs, legumes and geophytes. The density of a grass mat helps to prevent the development of other plant seedlings. The composition of a grassland and the dominant grass species vary with location and respond

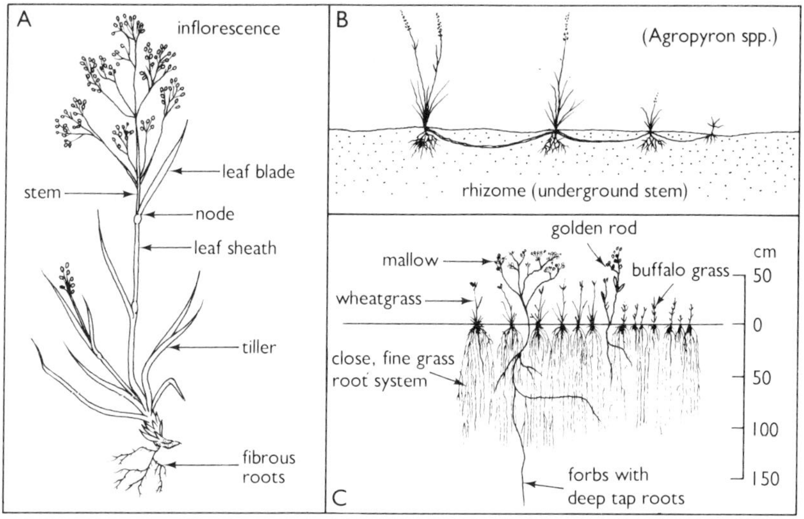

Fig. 3 A shows the structure of a typical annual grass; B the progressive development of shoots and new growth from a horizontal rhizome, whose decay may leave separate plants; C the density and depth of the fibrous roots of prairie grasses and tap roots of typical forbs.

to the available moisture. The better-watered grasslands tend to carry taller grasses with deeper, well-developed root systems, and give way to shorter grasses in more arid environments. This is a very broad generalisation, however, and the composition is never a response to any single variable. In some places there are many shrubs, in others numerous mosses and lichens. Many variables affect the plant–soil system in any particular place, and a broad grassland formation is really a mosaic made up of numerous component parts, each of which should really be examined in isolation. In practice, widespread quadrat sampling is needed to give a realistic picture of an extensive temperate grassland. Also its appearance is continuously changing—not only as the new green gives way to the buff colours of mature and withering grasses, but also with the appearance and disappearance of flowers developed from bulbs, such as iris, or from herbs, such as salvias, or compositae (daisies).

Grasses can often live where a moderate, or low precipitation and high evapo-transpiration do not permit tree growth, for their dense spreading roots can obtain nutrients from a shallow moist zone. The larger trees and shrubs have a greater water requirement, and need a longer growing season for tissue formation; whereas herbaceous plants can rapidly complete their life cycles. The spreading root systems and their ability to recover from grazing and burning give grasses an advantage in competition with most forbs. There are thus parts of the temperate lands where grasses have come to dominate large areas.

b) Distribution

Fig. 4 shows the distribution of the temperate grasslands, though most of the area formerly covered by wild vegetation is now either cultivated or used for controlled grazing. They go by various names: 'prairie' (*Fr.*, meadow), 'steppe' (where the genus *Stipa* is common), 'pampa' (*Sp.*, grassland), 'veld' (*Dutch*, grass). However, these terms are usually applied to specific areas and not necessarily to the whole grassland formation. The American tall-grass 'prairies' give way, as the land rises, to short-grass 'high plains'. On the other hand the Eurasian 'steppes' are often taken to include the steppe-heaths of central Europe and the far-distant 'steppes' east of Lake Baikal, whose flora include Alpine elements.

There are transitional zones, difficult to define—moister areas where grassland and stretches of forest intermingle, and those where dry grassland gives way to semi-desert flora. In some places, due to climatic or biotic influences, grassland has relatively recently replaced other types of vegetation. Even before man's large-scale interference, the grassland plants were continuously affected by the attentions of large numbers of herbivores. Thus even those limited areas which are now maintained as reserves of 'original vegetation' may not truly represent the plant communities of former times. Certainly man's interference with the wild animal population has affected the whole ecological balance. The destruction of the huge buffalo herds of North America and the modification of the habitats of prairie rodents, which consume large quantities of plant matter, have irreparably disturbed integral parts of the ecosystem. For these reasons the particular characteristics of the various continental grasslands are considered separately (p. 30).

The temperate grasslands of the northern hemisphere extend mainly over the continental interiors, between semi-arid zones and more humid, forested land. They cover such extensive surfaces of low relief that conditions vary gradually, but considerably, between these marginal areas. As the climates vary, so do their influences on soil formation. Parent rocks and surface deposits also influence soil characteristics, so that there are many different soil types within these large areas. However, rather than consider the numerous regional variations, it is better to look in turn at the external variables affecting plant/soil systems and see how they interact to produce the characteristics of a particular stretch of grassland.

In the southern hemisphere warm temperate grasslands, the pampas, extend westwards from the moist Atlantic coastland, between 32° and 35°S, to where semi-arid *monte* scrub covers the drier interior. To the south, the cooler, dry Patagonian region bears tussock grasses and xerophytic plants.

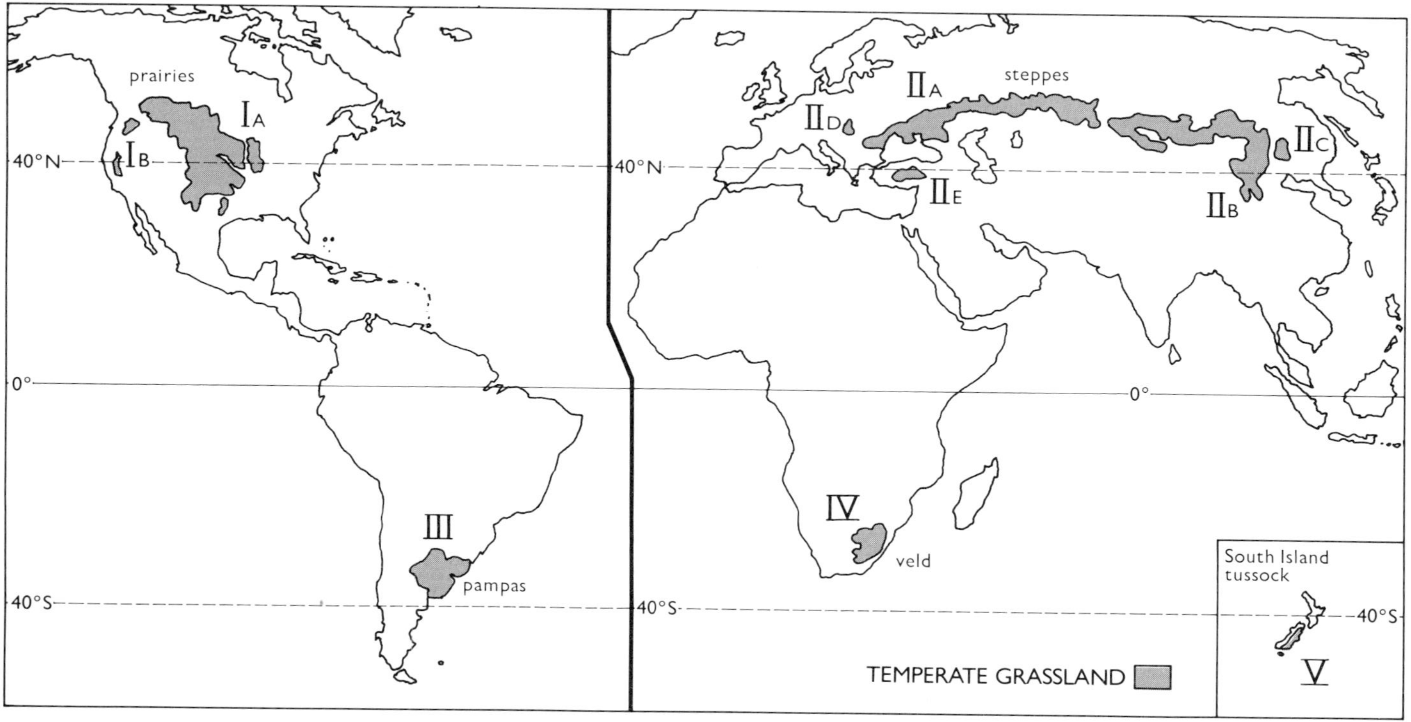

Fig. 4 Temperate Grasslands: IA Prairies/High Plains; IB Western bunch-grass. IIA Steppes; IIB Mongolian short-grass steppe; IIC Manchurian steppe; IID East European steppe; IIE Dry steppe; III Pampas; IV Veld; V Tussock grassland.

Fig. 5 Ploughing the deep black soils of the western steppes, where the grassland plants and steppe mat make up a biomass of some 20–50 tonnes per hectare. The silty soils, no longer protected by the turf mat, dry quickly; tree belts help to minimise moisture loss (Fig. 26).

The high plateau and mountain slopes of the eastern interior of South Africa is also covered by grassland (veld); though northwards, and below about 1000 m, the increasing proportion of shrubs and trees earns it the name 'bushveld', and it may be regarded as a south-eastern extension of the tropical savannas (Fig. 27). Similarly, most of Australia's extra-tropical wheat and stock lands have been developed by clearing savanna-like grass–tree–shrub associations. The small areas of tussock grassland in the east of New Zealand's South Island are difficult to account for purely on climatic grounds.

External Variables
I Climatic Influences

Plant Responses and Micro-climates

Grasses have a particularly strong competitive advantage over trees where there is a relatively low annual precipitation, with a summer maximum accompanied by high evapo-transpiration. The composition of the temperate grasslands tends to change with decreasing annual precipitation, for the production of plant tissue is closely related to the rainfall. The better-watered areas support tall-grass prairie, or 'steppe meadow', but the proportion of above-ground material tends to decrease along the moisture gradient, towards the drier lands. But even where the water content of the upper soil is low, the grass roots still form a spreading fibrous system and other herbs put down long tap roots; so that the drier grasslands also have a high proportion of root matter, and the overall biomass of the various grasslands varies less than one might imagine.

The grasses and other herbs create a great amount of litter, whose decomposition releases potential nutrients to the soil. The high proportion of worms and other small fauna in the moister regions help to mix the soil particles and nutrients, and also create spaces which contain oxygen needed by bacteria and other plant decomposers (p. 21). The rate of organic decomposition is at its highest in spring and early summer, yet even then it is usually slower than the rate of supply of organic material. This tends to produce a thick, matted sod, whose mass may exceed that of the plant material above ground.

The physical and micro-climatic influences of grassland plants and the matted layer are important. They intercept a high proportion of the rainfall, though some reaches the surface by stem-flow. As evapo-transpiration rates are high in summer, percolation into and through the soil is restricted. As the growing plants take up solutions, they affect the depth and duration of moisture within the soil, and may create a water deficit quite close to the surface. However, the close mat helps to protect the surface particles from wind and sheet wash.

The herbaceous layers interfere with direct insolation and with radiation losses from the soil surface. At maximum growth much insolation is reflected—a close prairie grassland may have an albedo of 15–25 per cent. The plants themselves then absorb a great deal of the incoming radiation before it reaches the soil surface. The height, density and composition of the vegetation affect the diurnal temperatures within

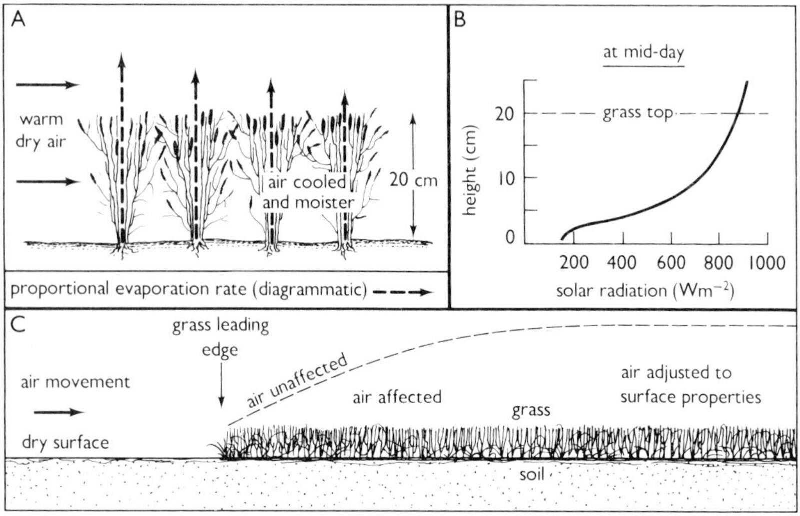

Fig. 6 Micro-climatic variations in an area of grassland: A stresses the difference between air over a dry heated surface and that within tall-grass, or a grain crop, which is hardly surprising as the transmission of short-wave radiation shows an almost logarithmic decay with depth of penetration (B). The extent of such modifications is indicated in C.[1]

the plant cover. On a summer's day the atmosphere near the ground surface remains cooler than near the top of a close plant cover; while at night the air temperature near the ground is generally higher than that near the top. Atmospheric humidity is often greater within close vegetation than in the free atmosphere, especially near the ground. Thus the plant organs develop in climatic conditions which are generally different from those in the free atmosphere.

The dense steppe meadows, where many of the forbs have horizontal leaf arrangements, give a fairly continuous ground cover, and produce micro-climates which favour very different plant forms and associations from those of the drier grasslands. Macro- and micro-climate conditions are thus interrelated; yet the latter may have important ecological effects, even in the more open, drier grassland, where near-surface temperatures beneath patches covered with low plants contrast with those near the exposed surface. Evaporation from the exposed surface helps to cause general soil aridity; yet dominant plants, once established, create protective micro-enviroments in which other plants may develop.

General Climatic Conditions

Most of the prairies and steppes have cold, or very cold winters. Air from the polar continental air masses surges outwards from time to time. In America, especially towards the south of the prairies, this may conflict with warmer, moister air and produce very variable conditions. In the northern parts, frost penetrates deeply and a snow cover usually remains until spring, even though precipitation amounts are generally small. The temperature rises quickly in spring, helped in North America by Chinook winds, which cause rapid snow-melt. Where the ground is slow to thaw, this may produce swampy conditions, but generally this is a time when water percolates most readily.

The summer temperatures in the continental interiors are high for the latitude, and relatively low pressures allow an influx of moist air. Convection causes heavy storms, and in the wetter parts of the grasslands periods of leaching transfer soluble minerals downwards through the soil. Generally, however, evapo-transpiration is high at this time, limiting percolation. Towards the interior the summer rainfall is less, and much more erratic. In the south-central USSR the influence of tropical continental air also causes very dry conditions, with high temperatures.

In summer, the northern margins have long periods of daylight compared with the southern parts. This means that the composition of their grassland communities varies, for short-day plants tend to be excluded from high latitudes and long-day plants from low latitudes; this is particularly evident in the North American prairies, with their great latitudinal extent. However, species of needlegrass (*Stipa*) and grama grass (*Bouteloua*) occur throughout.

In all the grasslands wind greatly affects the soils and vegetation, by increasing evapo-transpiration, drying out the soil, and removing loose particles. It also plays a major role in dispersing small, light seeds.

Broad Variations within the Grasslands

Although a close study of any particular grassland area should involve micro-meteorological observations, the mean figures for selected locations shown in Fig. 8 give a broad view of the conditions favouring various types of temperate grassland.

North American Prairies The prairies stretch from about 55°N to south of 30°N. In the USA these temperate grasslands cover plains which, in general, become drier as they rise westwards to some 1500 m above sea-level. The mean temperatures and evaporation rates tend to rise towards the south. Fig. 8 gives data for the four places shown in Fig. 7.

D is in a region where the tall-grass prairie is floristically rich, abundant with herbs, and bright with flowers in the moist mid-summer[2]. Grasses, like the big bluestems (*Andropogon gerardi*), are 1–2 m tall and have a dense root network. They form a continuous sward and flower late. Here the rich soils remain moist to a considerable depth.

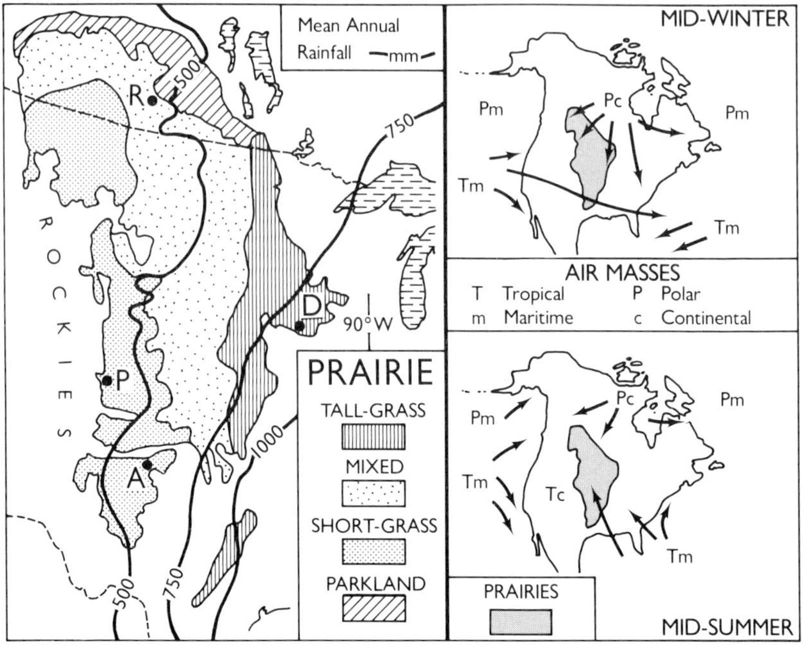

Fig. 7 While observing the apparent relationship between precipitation and grassland distributions, remember that the influences of altitude, latitude and soil materials are significant. The flows from airmass sources are typical of these seasons, but variations in their occurrence and persistence often affect soil-vegetation stability. (R Regina, D Des Moines, P Pueblo, A Amarillo.)

In the prairies about R and A many short sward-forming grasses, like grama, wheatgrass (*Agropyron*) and buffalo grass (*Buchloe dactyloides*), mingle with the taller ones. Both the low winter temperature in the north and the dryness of the winter in the south enforce long rest periods. At R rapid snow-melt provides water for spring growth, while at A much of the rain falls in scattered heavy storms in the spring and summer months, though at these times evaporation rates are high.

At P on the higher, but dry, western plains, there is short-grass prairie, usually with fewer species of herbaceous plants; here, in any case, grazing kills out grasses of middle height. Again, it must be stressed that throughout the prairies the former vegetation has been modified by grazing, cultivation and fire, and that the grasslands are an open system where ready adjustments to disturbances, and local soil conditions, create a mosaic of varied plant associations. In the even drier marginal lands, grasses tend to form clumps or tussocks, and sagebrush and various xerophytic plants appear, with bare patches between.

The same general east-west variations occur in Canada, though short-grass associations are found in the dry parts of the south-central prairies, with a belt of taller grasses forming a crescent about them.

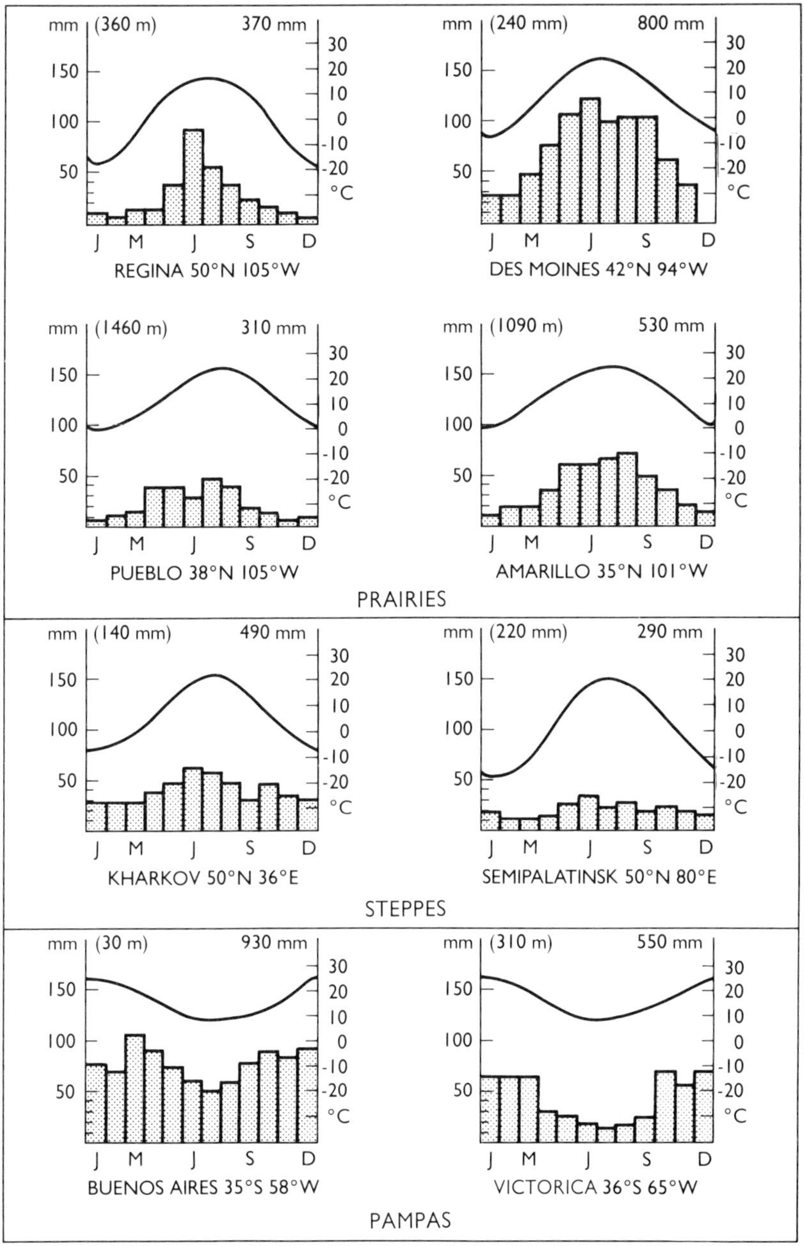

Fig. 8 Mean annual precipitation and air temperatures for selected places within the prairies (Fig. 7), steppes (Fig. 15), and pampas. Notice the influences of continentality and of latitude in the case of the prairies, and the relative mildness of the pampas.

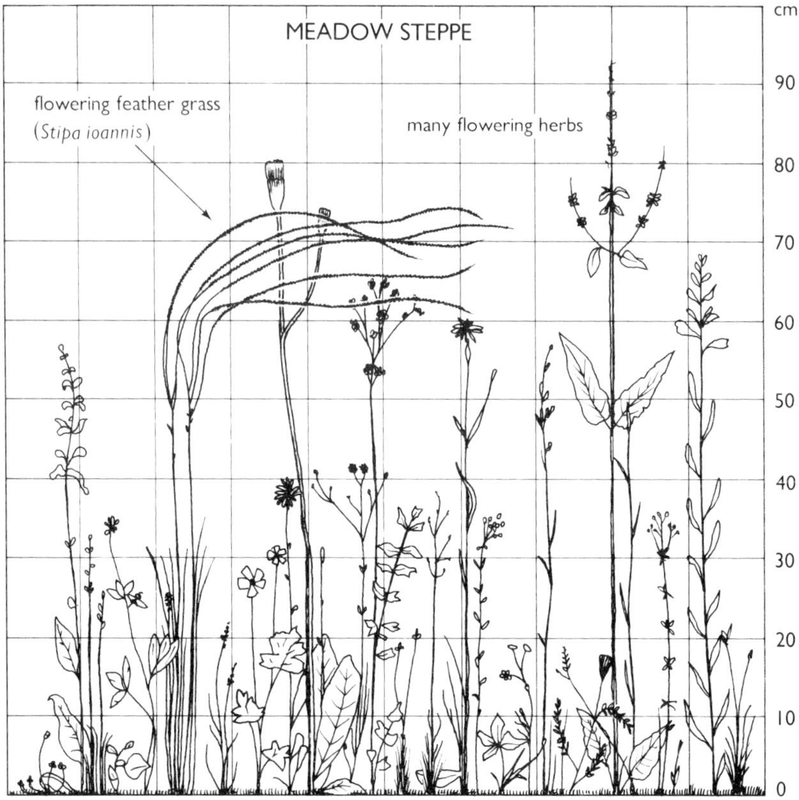

Fig. 9 A meadow steppe in early summer, showing the association of grasses and herbs, many in flower. (After Walter.[3])

The Eurasian Steppes These have less latitudinal spread than the North American prairies, but extend from eastern Europe far across central Asia at about latitude 50°N. The aridity tends to increase from north-west to south-east, as the precipitation decreases and summer temperatures and potential evaporation rise. In the cooler, moister north and west there is a relatively short, dry period. Here grasses and tree seedlings compete, and patches of forest and steppe intermingle[3]. Fig. 8 gives data for Kharkov, located where the original meadow steppe of mat-forming grasses resembled the tall-grass prairie. Southwards and eastwards, where the precipitation is lower and winter drought more pronounced, the grassland is dominated by tufted *Stipa*, together with other shorter turf-forming grasses. Data for Semipalatinsk (Figs. 8 and 15) show that towards the interior conditions are drier still and the annual temperature range greater; here shorter turf-forming grasses, such as *Festuca sulcata*, are dominant. They give way to dry tussock and xerophytic shrubs in the semi-arid lands. Far away to the east are the short-grass steppes of Mongolia.

The Pampas In the maritime north-east of these warm temperate lands there is an annual rainfall of some 1000 mm. But, with high temperatures and winds blowing freely across the grasslands, the potential evaporation is very high, and exceeds the rainfall in all but the La Plata coastal region. The rainfall is fairly evenly distributed throughout the year, though in January and February it falls in sharp storms on only about seven days each month. At this time the daylight radiation is intense, so that the vegetation dries rapidly. The rainfall diminishes towards the south and west, being about 500 mm at the dry interior limits of the pampas, where the true grasslands give way to low, deciduous, broad-leafed trees and xerophytic bushes (*monte*).

Little remains of the original pampa vegetation of tall bunch-grasses (*Melic* spp.), for European grasses and lucerne have been introduced for grazing. The soils in the moister parts have a thick humus horizon, which provides evidence of the former tall-grass species, of many herbs, and a lack of trees—conditions which resemble those of the mid-prairies. The dry south-west supports natural tussock grassland, with *Stipa* species and few herbs. The mild winters favour such tussock development, in which young leaves develop among the remains of the old withered ones.

Conditions on the temperate grasslands of the high tablelands of South Africa are described on p. 40.

Climatic Variability and Vegetation Responses

The grassland environment is intermediate between arid and humid climates, and usually has an annual moisture deficiency. The precipitation varies considerably from year to year, especially towards the drier parts. A period with unusually high rainfall may be followed by a number of drought years. The prairies, for instance, are occasionally subjected to abnormally long periods of strong westerly airflows, so that humid air moving northwards from the Gulf of Mexico is diverted eastwards. Westerly winds normally affect the prairies in winter, but when they persist for most of the year droughts occur.

In western Kansas, a period of 76 years included 36 per cent of the months with drought, 36 per cent wetter than average, and only 12 per cent near the statistical mean. Following six wet years, the period 1932–40 was exceptionally dry, with some extreme droughts. Strong winds created severe dust storms. During the wet years there had been an increase of medium- and tall-grasses, which formed an upper storey over short-grasses, but during the long drought, even the ground cover of short-grasses was reduced from 80–90 per cent to 20 per cent. A few grasses survived at first—big bluestem (*Andropogon*) by virtue of deep roots, and *Stipa spartia* by rolling its leaves and becoming dormant.

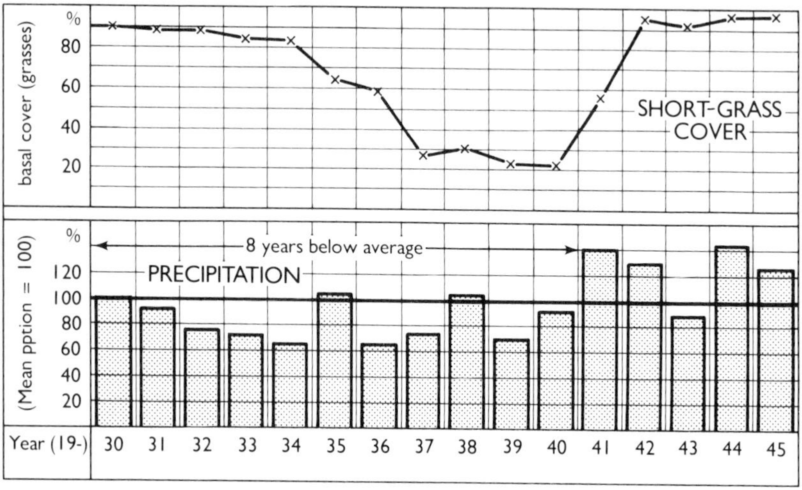

Fig. 10 Annual precipitation on the prairies of Kansas. Notice the variability and the long drought between 1930–41, when, except for two years, the rainfall was below average. The progressive deterioration of the grasslands, and their recovery, are shown above.

Grasshoppers increased in the dry conditions and helped to eliminate plants. Most grasses failed to bloom, and, like the forbs, almost disappeared, while xerophytic plants, including cacti, spread[4].

The Eurasian steppes are subject to similar fluctuations between droughts and wetter periods. The western steppes also experienced drought conditions between 1934–39. The steppes east of the Volga,

Fig. 11 Strong winds have caused severe soil loss from this farmland east of the Ukraine, and created dust storms. Young barley has been so affected (pecked line) that additional sowing is needed.

which straddle the boundary between Siberia and Kazakhstan, were developed between 1954–61 under the 'Virgin Lands' reclamation scheme, but have since suffered from the unreliable rainfall; there were serious droughts in 1963 and 1975.

There are also long-term fluctuations in the vegetation composition. Evidence that in post-glacial times the boundaries between tall-grass steppe and deciduous forest have shifted comes from the presence of deserted burrows of steppe rodents beneath the present forest.

Climate and Soil Formation

Those soils developed under grass which retain a soft, generally dark, surface horizon, and are basic, are classified as Mollisols. Among these are the black earths (czernozems) which underlie much of the moister temperate grasslands. Where the climate becomes drier, they grade into dark chestnut-brown soils and then into pale brown soils, which contain much less organic matter.

As the grasses die down, a thick turf mat accumulates. Beneath this the dense, fine root system decays and provides humus within the soil. This helps to produce a granular, crumby structure, and aerates the upper part. Large quantities of nutrients are extracted by the grasses, and returned as litter which produces humus sufficiently dark to give the soil a blackish cover. Sometimes humus fills the burrows of small animals. Worms and other soil fauna mix the organic and mineral matter.

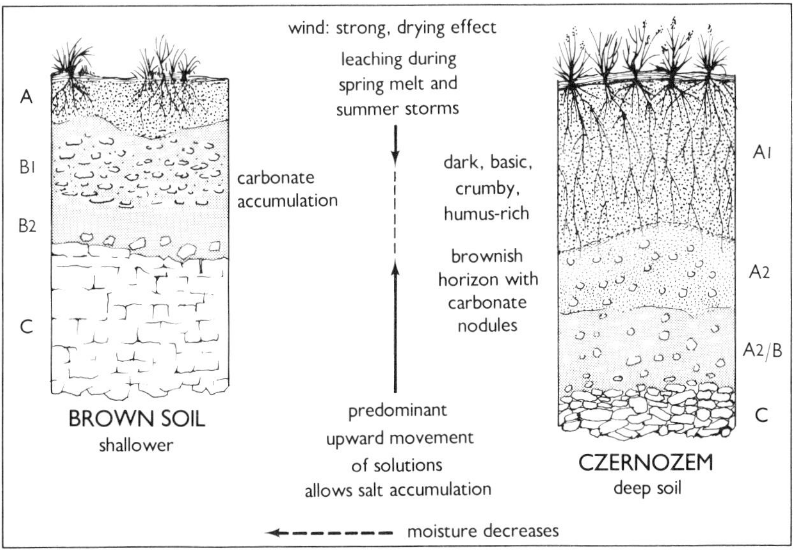

Fig. 12 Notice the differences in depth, structure and content of the A–B horizons of the black and brown grassland soils.[5]

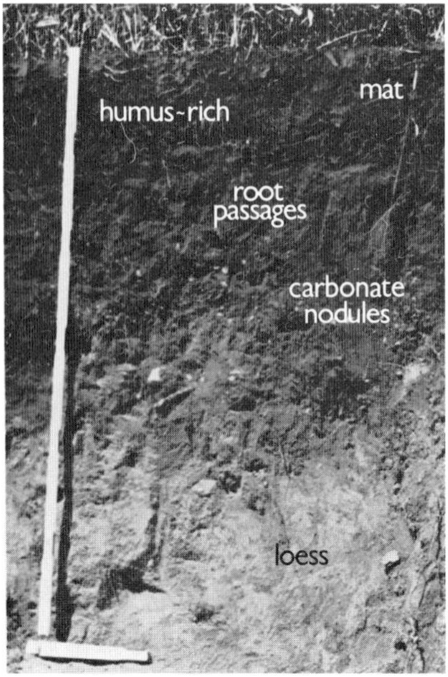

Fig. 13 A deep czernozem developed in prairie loess.

Only during the spring snow-melt and after heavy summer storms is there downward percolation and leaching to any depth. In summer, both the rapid evaporation and transpiration from grasses and forbs bring up soil solutions. As the upward movement of solutions persists, the less soluble salts, such as calcium carbonate, accumulate. These dark soils have a high pH value, and under basic conditions the clay compounds do not readily dissociate. Fig. 12 shows the thick dark A level developed above a lighter horizon where calcium carbonate, occasionally leached down, remains as nodules or concretions, above the weathering parent material. The drier the conditions, the nearer the carbonate-rich horizon to the surface.

Such profiles are developed upon a variety of parent rocks able to support grassland. The unconsolidated calcareous sediments, such as loess, which occurs widely beneath the temperate grasslands, are particularly favourable. The shallow brown soils of the drier grasslands, with less organic matter, have calcareous deposits in the upper horizon, and so tend to be prismatic, friable and basic. They deteriorate rapidly if over-grazed or otherwise mismanaged.

On the wetter margins of the tall-grass prairies, where more frequent precipitation allows more percolation and leaching, calcium carbonate does not accumulate. But pH values, though lower, are still between 6.5 and 7.0, and humus is abundant. Somewhat confusingly, these dark, mineral-rich soils, transitional between pedocals and pedalfers, are known as 'Prairie Soil' (Fig. 14).

Climatic Hazards and Agriculture

The unreliability of rainfall and lengthy droughts are still a threat to cultivators and stock farmers. Water storages, for irrigation purposes, numerous small stock dams, and soil water conservation techniques help to prevent major disasters (p. 32), though short-term losses can still be great (p. 44). Tornadoes and summer convectional storms with hail can devastate wheat crops, and in America insurance rates against hail are high. During winter, heavy snow storms can prevent grazing and isolate stock from fodder supplies, even towards the south of the prairies.

II The Influences of Local Rocks

Much of the temperate grassland vegetation has developed on a mantle of material transported by wind (loess), or by ice sheets (moraine, often resorted by water), or by river floods (alluvium); so that the underlying rocks often have only a minor influence on vegetation characteristics, and the soils are developed from a wide range of mixed

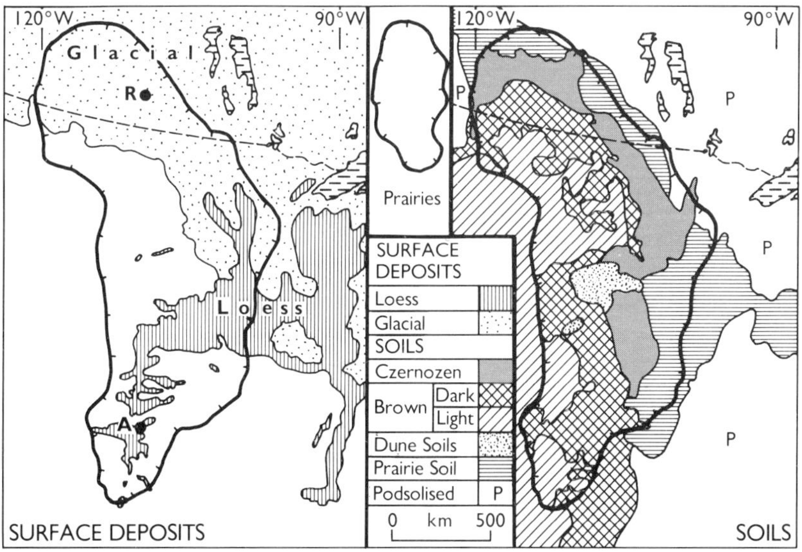

Fig. 14 Notice how much of the grassland was developed on surface deposits of loess or glacial material, where there is a high proportion of the deeper, moister soils. The scale emphasises the huge extent of the prairies. (R Regina, A Amarillo.)

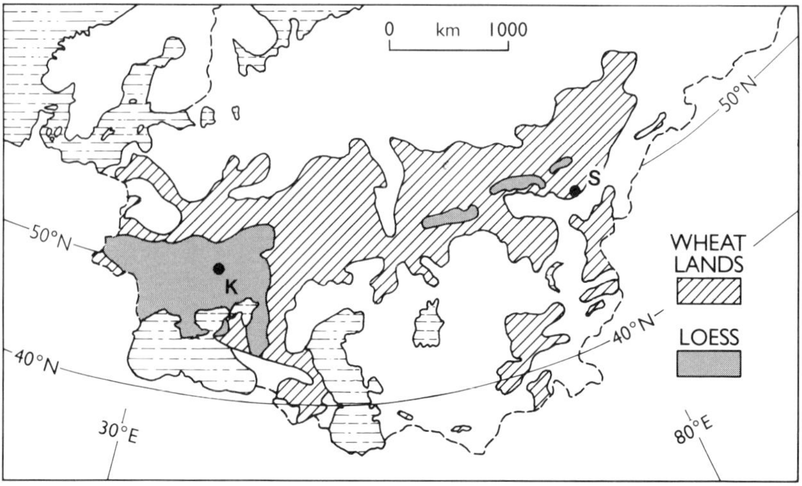

Fig. 15 Loess is the parent material beneath most of the western steppes, where mixed farming is now established. Climatic differences between the western and eastern grasslands are shown by the mean figures for Kharkov (K) and Semipalatinsk (S) in Fig. 8.

minerals. For instance, those of the northern prairies are formed mainly from glacial deposits, while south of the Missouri many parts of the plains are covered by almost continuous deposits of loess. However, on the high plains much of the grassland covers Tertiary sandstones derived from the mountains. In the USSR the gently tilted Tertiaries and intrusive volcanics of the Ukrainian steppes are covered by thick loess, which also lies over sedimentary rocks in parts of northern Kazakhstan, in the drier eastern steppelands.

In general, soils developed on fine, deep, transported material which retains water favour a close grass cover rather than trees. Absorption by a network of grass roots is an efficient means of taking up water and nutrients from unconsolidated deposits. By contrast, coarse, permeable parent material, which allows rapid water percolation and deep tree root penetration, is less likely to bear grassy sward.

Other basic rocks, beside loess, may weather to support grassland—among them basalts and diorites, fine-grained calcareous sandstones and marls. On limestones soils may develop in the accumulations of residual particles left as the carbonate weathers away. But though grasses maintain an active calcium cycle with such soils, calcium in large concentrations may chemically interfere with the supply of other nutrients to plants.

A glacial mantle often provides a varied surface with clayey hollows, which fill with water, and patches of less fertile outwash; while river systems crossing the plains may cut into a loose mantle of moraine or loess and expose rocks beneath. In some places, gently tilted surfaces terminate in a broken scarp standing above a lower, flat sedimentary plain—as on the wide, stepped plains of the Canadian prairies. There are often trees and shrubs on such slopes, sometimes due to one dominant factor, but more often to a combination of causes, such as relative freedom from grazing or fires, shelter from persistent wind, greater soil mobility or perhaps the absence of a thick turf mat. Thus there is a variety of physical features and vegetation within the grasslands.

In moister locations, coarse, sandy material tends to produce more acidic, podsolic soils. In the Nebraska Sand Hills the breakdown of Tertiary sandstones, redistributed by wind, produced extensive areas of loose material, with large tracts of dunes. The soils are generally acidic, immature and absorb water; they are underlain by aquifers and enclose ponds and marshes, and support a variety of grasses. Today, chemically improved, they support sown, irrigated cattle pastures[6].

In general, though consolidated parent rocks may be of local significance, they have only minor influence on the broad distribution of the temperate grasslands. Transported materials, giving a wide choice of mixed minerals, are of greater significance, while the grassland characteristics, and the nature of the soils, owe much to climatic controls and the effects of herbivores and fires.

III The Biosphere—a Variety of Influences

Earthworms, ants and numerous insects help to mix the soils beneath the grasslands. Each square metre of upper soil has hundreds of worm passages, and worms affect the soil profile several metres beneath the surface. Together, their activities create the space and aeration which allow the bacteria and microfauna to decompose the organic matter.

Animals and Grassland Ecology

The open grasslands afford little protection for the bigger animals. The large herbivores usually herd together for protection, and continuously migrate to avoid the over-use of forage. There are fewer dominant species of large mammals than on the tropical grasslands. They include the buffalo and pronghorn antelope of North America, the wild horse and

Fig. 16 In a few decades the decimation of the great herds of buffalo changed the whole ecological balance of the grassland.

saiga antelope of Asia, the guanaco of the pampas, and the various antelopes of the veld.

The prairies, as a whole, once supported tens of millions of bison, millions of pronghorn on the drier grasslands, and elk near the grass–woodland margins[7]. On the present rangelands it is still possible to detect buffalo tracks to rivers and wallows. Their grazing, the impact of hooves, and their droppings have all affected the ecology of the grasslands, as have the activities of other animals. The bison and prairie dogs (burrowing rodents) have tended to change both the *Andropogon*-dominated tall-grass land and the mixed prairies into short-grass associations. The boundary between the principal grass types has fluctuated both with the rainfall and the number of herbivores. The other burrowing rodents include ground squirrels, gophers, mice and kangaroo rats. They all bring enormous amounts of material to the surface. The prairie dogs dig 3–4 m deep, but live in separate territorial colonies so that their effects are more local than those of the ground squirrels. Badgers are also widespread and dig for rodents.

Jack rabbits live on the short-grasses and use the taller for shelter, for predators like the wolf and coyote can also live in open grassland. A complicated food web exists. Mice, voles and ground squirrels not only eat seeds and bulbs but also grasshoppers, crickets, beetles, and spiders, which are all abundant. The numbers and biomass of insects are huge; they are also consumed by birds, which include larks, sparrows, pippits and the larger prairie chicken. Snakes feed on lizards, frogs, toads and worms—some on squirrels and voles.

Fig. 17 Prairie dogs have rapidly multiplied with the destruction of predators; burrows such as this devastate grassland and lead to erosion.

Wildlife–Grassland Co-evolution

Selective grazing by mammals has long controlled the composition of the plant communities. The grassland turf mat acts as a nutrient store, conserving soil moisture, and preventing casual seeding by other plants, including tree species. Intruding, outstanding seedlings are likely to be spotted and eaten by grazing animals. In places, over-grazing and trampling must have broken the turf mat; but, on the whole, a balance was established which allowed grasslands and herbivores to co-evolve.

In open systems like these, fluctuations in annual populations reverberate through the interacting variables. For instance, a decrease in the number of predators can lead to an increase in the number of burrowing animals, with consequent deterioration of the grassland surface, and a decrease in the smaller life-forms on which the burrowers prey. Such population fluctuations seem to happen from time to time in the wild, initiated perhaps by climatic-vegetational changes, or by animal diseases, or by aggression when animal societies become over-populous. Men undoubtedly initiated such a chain by killing wolves and coyotes on the prairies, and big game and predators on the steppes; they have since experienced the effects of myriads of rodents on soils and crops.

Man's direct influences on the temperate grasslands have been so drastic that we must first consider the general results of his interference before looking in more detail at the land-use and settlement patterns which have largely replaced the natural vegetation.

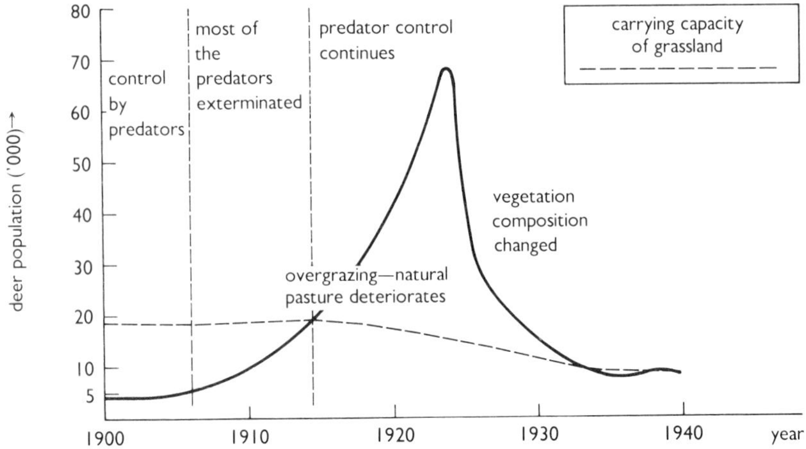

Fig. 18 Fluctuations in deer population in northern Arizona.[8] The destruction of the animals which preyed on them allowed the deer to increase, so that in a few years they greatly exceeded the carrying capacity of the rapidly deteriorating grassland. Starvation drastically reduced the population, until the numbers fluctuated about the new capacity of the pastures, affected by climatic variations.

Fire

In fact, fires may be started by lightning or volcanic activity, as well as by man. It is difficult to assess the extent to which fire due to natural causes has affected the grasslands. Man has long fired the grass, either accidentally, or to clear land, or to eliminate dead vegetation and promote new growth[8]. North American Indians certainly modified the vegetation by using fire to flush game and renew forage. Wind sweeps fire rapidly across the grassland; and fire favours grasses at the expense of shrubs and trees. But while grasses recover quickly and grow more vigorously, trees may lose many years' growth, and, once eliminated, do not establish themselves easily. This is true even in the moister areas, where grasses often establish a firm organic mat. Strong wind may increase the intensity of fire to the extent that it dries and ignites the soil's organic material and damages underground plant organs; but generally fire has been an important factor in extending and maintaining areas of grassland.

Man Manipulates the Energy Flow

Fig. 19 shows the energy flow along a chain developed on the natural grassland, with the area of the boxes proportional to the biomass. The grasses and other plants are *producers* which accumulate energy from the sun. Much of this is stored in the biomass, but a great deal is lost

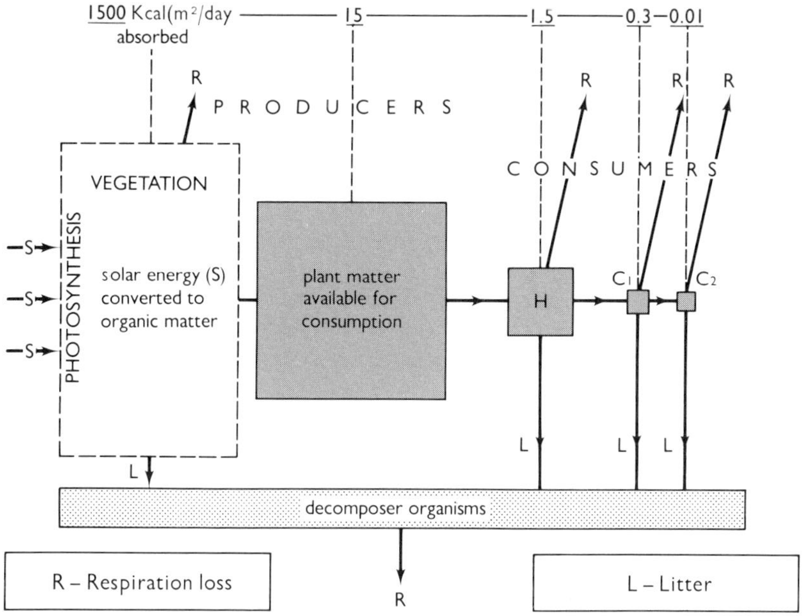

Fig. 19 The figures, which assume that some 1500 Kcals of solar energy per square metre are absorbed each day and converted to organic matter, show that the net available energy becomes less at each level away from the plant producers, as herbivore H is consumed by carnivore C_1. which falls prey to carnivore C_2. The energy losses due to respiration and decomposers are shown, but imports and exports of energy and organic matter, into and out of the system, are omitted.

through respiration, and so leaves the system. Much dies and forms litter on the surface. When grass is eaten by a herbivore (*consumer*) the energy is transferred to a new stage, or trophic, level, into the biomass of the animal, which expends energy in foraging and in maintaining its body temperature; it may in time add its remains to the litter. The litter is broken down by decomposer organisms, which play a key role in recycling nutrients: much energy is also lost from the system in this process. The herbivore may be consumed by a carnivore, which also expends energy; so that the net energy available gets less at each level away from the producer. These transfers are shown in Fig. 19, which assumes that no energy, other than solar energy, enters. This is not always the case.

Man may manipulate the ecosystem to his advantage. More energy will be available if he acts as a herbivore rather than as a carnivore. He ensures that unwanted producers—weeds—are removed, and concentrates productivity in a grain crop or a few pasture plant species. In the latter case he seeks a supply of animal nutrients, protein and animal by-products, rather than a high energy return through starchy

Fig. 20 Dry grassland with sagebrush in an area of erratic rainfall near the New Mexico–Texas border, part of the early ranch lands. Now Herefords can be supported by irrigated fodder crops.

plants. So his pastures must be as productive as possible and the stock as efficient converters as possible. He therefore introduces energy to the system—to drive machinery, run transport, manufacture implements, fertilisers and pesticides, provide irrigation, drainage and so on. His input of energy per calorie of food output is often very high. On the world's large temperate grasslands it has been increasing with the years. In 1910 the USA put in about a calorie of energy for each calorie of food output. By 1930 the input was three calories; by 1960 six calories; and by 1980 it was almost ten calories.

Progressive Development of the Grasslands

Man's impact on the major grasslands has varied with the history of settlement, with the introduction of new technologies, and with demands for meat and grain from distant consumers. We see this clearly in the development of the American grasslands, and can observe comparable stages of development in the others.

The Prairies These were relatively little disturbed by man until the early 16th century, when North American Indians began to use the horses introduced by Spaniards to hunt buffalo[9]. Even so, the pressure on the animals and the soils of tribal territories were slight. Even in the 19th century when white Americans began to cross the prairies in numbers from the east, their destinations were agricultural lands in Oregon, or

Fig. 21 Inputs which have transformed the natural grassland are reflected in the ordered landscape in Saskatchewan with roads, railways, a mine and chemical works which produce potash, used in fertilisers.

gold in California, or silver in the Rockies, and the treeless plains were regarded as a difficult barrier. The dryness of the prairies inhibited farmers whose technologies were adapted to the humid eastern lands. There was a lack of building materials: the early buildings were of grass sods, with turf roofs. The surface water was limited, seasonal and erratic. Their first clashes with the Indians came through their activities as buffalo hunters, with firearms, or through protecting westward-bound wagon trains.

But next came the ranchers. They operated first in Texas, where horsemen moved their almost wild longhorn cattle over open ranges. By the 1870s, as the railways pushed westwards across middle America, stock was driven northwards along forage routes, to be trucked to cities on the eastern rim of the prairies—St Louis, Kansas City, Chicago. The stock was improved, and ranching spread northwards to the grasslands of Montana and western Canada.

The 1880s brought barbed wire and enclosures, to help stock breeding and protect crops, for cultivation was spreading westwards, and the humid plains now supported homesteads which farmed allocated blocks of 65 or 130 hectares each. Varieties of grain were being developed to suit dry farming techniques and were better able to withstand frost and drought, though yields were low by modern standards. Mechanisation and the use of windpumps helped agricultural settlement to advance westwards, spurred on by the increasing demands of world-wide markets.

Meanwhile, firearms had been used to devastate the great herds of buffalo and pronghorns, and to overcome Indian resistance; and fierce clashes between cattlemen and advancing farmers had forced the ranching on to the drier, rougher western plains. The grasslands had been transformed[10]: but the new ecological balances were precarious and ever-shifting. The removal of the natural grass-cover exposed the soils to the risk of serious erosion. In climatically good years their natural fertility tempted settlers to extend wheat-growing to dry lands, too far west. The dry years brought disasters: the droughts of the nineties were a largely unheeded warning of the devastation caused by the long droughts of the 1930s, when countless millions of tonnes of once fertile top-soil were lost from the great western 'dust bowl'.

The original holdings were really too small for extensive farming, and in bad times the lack of capital and inadequate equipment proved disastrous for a system based on monoculture. The ranching areas, too, suffered from the unwillingness to adjust the numbers of stock to the varying climatic conditions. Over-grazing caused grasslands to deteriorate, and as their carrying capacity fell, sheep and goats often replaced the cattle.

Since the critical situation of the thirties, there have been many changes and improvements, though climatic hazards still cause local distress [11]. The farms have become larger; and capital for development is more readily available from outside the region, which helps to tide over bad periods. The construction of many large reservoirs and numerous small stock dams enables farmers to irrigate pastures and fodder crops and so increase cattle density. Grain growers benefit by using crop strains developed to suit local conditions and stand up to expected climatic variations. Contour ploughing and the use of shelter crops now help preserve soil stability. Crop diversification and rotation lessen the dangers of monoculture. A huge increase in sorghum-growing on former wheatfields produces high value stock feed. More energy is now introduced in the forms of mechanisation, fertilisers and pesticides. But these, like the use of aircraft for pasture seeding and crop spraying, and the employment of teams of harvesters are large inputs, which means that the farmer looks for a correspondingly high return on investment.

Thus the nature of extensive farming has altered, with the use of local intensive practices. There have not only been practical innovations, but also a reduction of farm labour, with consequent social changes. Alternative employment is needed to check outward migration from the prairies. The distribution of urban and industrial settlements, and employment opportunities, differ in the prairies of the USA and Canada. In the USA, both the sparsely-populated ranchlands and the more closely-settled prairie farmlands have sent their produce to flour mills and meat-packing plants in the big cities on the eastern margins. The small prairie settlements lie in the distributive hinterland of such huge cities as Minneapolis and Kansas City. In Canada, however, the large eastern cities are separated from the prairies by the forests and lakes of the southern Shield. Railways carry huge quantities of grain from local elevators to export terminals and mills at the eastern and western ports; but prairie towns like Edmonton, Calgary, Regina, and Saskatoon have agricultural processing factories and other industries, which provide employment within the grasslands. The friction of distance acts to encourage manufacturing to supply local demands. Also, in the case of Edmonton and Calgary, the oil, petro-chemical industries and ancillary engineering have helped to provide employment. By contrast, the central prairies of the USA have remained largely non-industrial.

Such progressive developments have replaced the ancestral plant associations of the natural temperate grasslands. Special conditions have preserved some grassland areas, and small reserves are maintained in places, as in eastern Kansas, where tall bluestem grasses remain on the stony limestones of the Flint Hills; this may become a tall-grass National Park[2]. Military areas in Saskatchewan have precariously preserved original plant associations and prairie animals[10]. It is vital to have reserves of such plants for genetic purposes (p. 45).

The Steppes The overall character of these grasslands changed little until the 18th century, though waves of nomadic tribes had spread over them from early times, and for centuries the whole of the western steppes

Fig. 22 Grain-growing has given way to more intensive mixed farming in the southern Ukraine: here water from the river Don is used for canal and sprinkler irrigation.

was dominated by the Khazans and then the Tartars. As in the American West, the first agricultural settlements were on the moister margins, where family groups of former serfs from the Russian state in the forested north established small scattered farms. The interior grasslands continued to support bands of nomadic Mongoloid horsemen.

During the 18th century many more settlers took to stock-rearing on the western steppes. Early in the 19th century large estates were established, with small peasant farms, operated by serfs. By the 1880s, most of the deep, fertile czernozems of the western loess lands were yielding huge quantities of winter wheat, much of it for export. At first, Russian expansion on to the eastern grasslands had been mainly to subdue the nomadic tribes; but now farm settlement spread to the eastern steppes beyond the Volga, and cattle and sheep grazed large areas of natural pasture. Here, with more severe winters, spring wheat was grown. But the hazards of droughts, dessicating winds, and summer storms became apparent when ploughs broke down the soil structure, and there was severe erosion.

In the west, the natural grassland was soon replaced by crops and sown pastures, and little remains today. The Ukraine now supports a more intensive form of land-use, with a wider range of crops. Besides wheat, there are sugar beet, sunflowers, potatoes, and fodder crops, and stock farming includes pigs as well as cattle. Diversification and the widespread use of the southward-flowing rivers for irrigation help to combat erosion, as does the use of strip farming, contour ploughing, and tree belts acting as wind-breaks. The cities and towns within the steppes have agriculturally-based industries.

The demands of increasing population led to the development of the 'Virgin Lands' of south-west Siberia and Kazakhstan, to exploit the fertility of chestnut-brown soils, built up under natural grassland, to produce spring wheat. Between 1954–61 immense areas were put under plough in this region of limited and erratic rainfall. Highly mechanised state farms produce huge quantities of grain, despite low yields per hectare. Periods of drought have since led to wind erosion. But here, too, schemes of irrigation, crop diversification and rotation systems have been introduced.

Thus the major wheat-producing region has shifted progressively east, and the former wheatlands have diversified their farming systems.

The Pampas As in America, the early colonists found little inducement to settle the temperate grasslands. The expanses of tall-grass pampas, occupied by nomadic Indians, were ignored by the Spaniards. However, from the 16th century, cattle and horses escaped from their riverside settlements and multiplied in the wild. The Indians made little direct impact on the grasslands, though their fires may have stimulated and

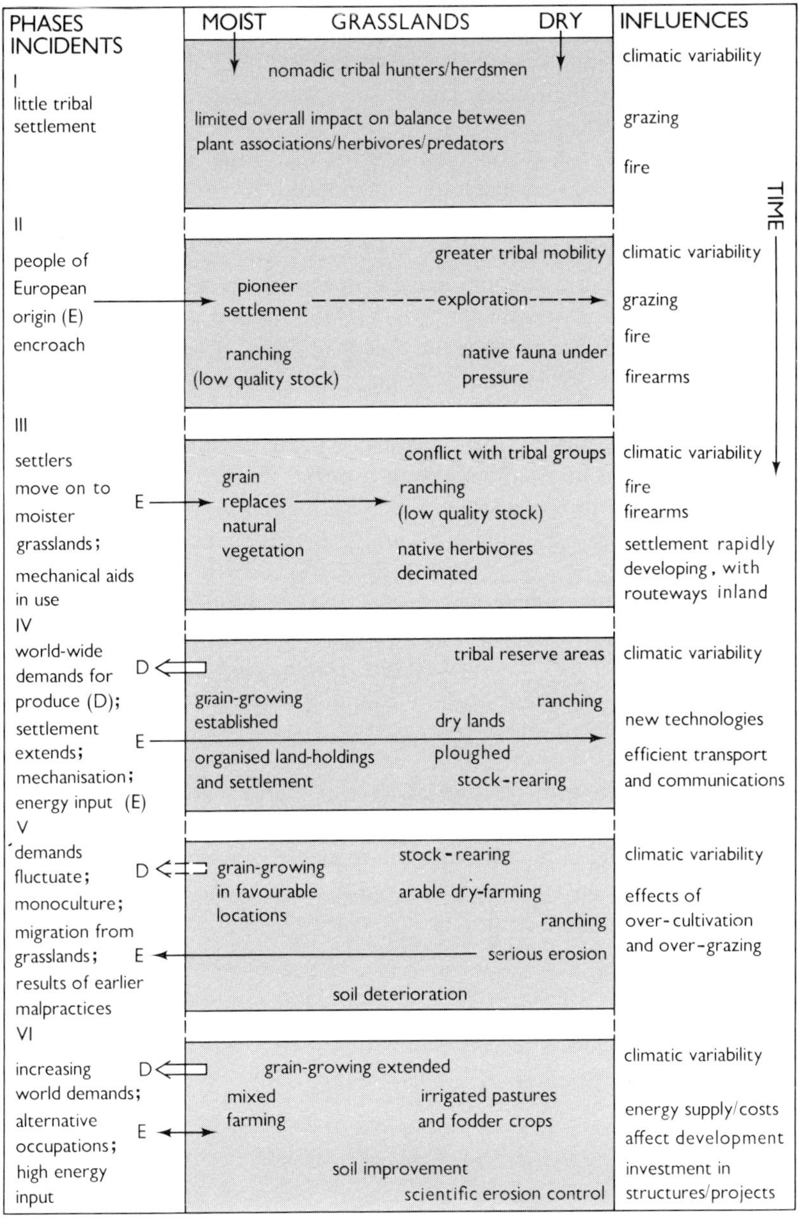

Fig. 23 The sequences of development of prairies, steppes and pampas by people of European origin had much in common. The grasslands were virtually extensive wastes to the early European-Americans, Spaniards of the Plate estuary, and peripheral Russian peoples. The progressive destruction of flora and fauna and displacement of earlier peoples are seen to be accompanied by increasing inputs of energy. Climatic variability is a continuous control; but modern settlement is influenced by demands and decisions far from the grasslands themselves.

perpetuated grass growth. By the 18th century, the excellent natural pastures supported some 40 million wild cattle, and individuals acquired rights to kill them for their hides. Horses, too, were tamed for cattle control and for transport.

By the start of the 19th century, salted meat was being exported, and British shorthorn cattle and sheep were introduced. As on the other grasslands, the situation began to change rapidly from the mid-19th century, when European demands for food were increasing. Foreign capital, from Britain in particular, and European immigrants, especially Italians, began to transform the pampas, and the Indians were relentlessly displaced. European cattle breeds required good feed, and immigrant share-croppers were used to plant lucerne (p. 42). Here, too, wire fencing and windpumps helped to control pastoral and arable farming. Railways fanned out from the major ports, as refrigerated storage and transport allowed large meat exports. The growth of wheat, maize and fodder crops increased enormously. Agricultural industries were established at the exporting ports and at places along the Parana and Uruguay rivers.

Through land grants, agricultural production came into the hands of relatively few landowners, though, by a complicated system of tenancy, they sub-divided parts of their huge estates. The division of the large properties and maintenance of profitable holdings of a suitable size are still land-use problems (p. 41).

The sequences of development which have converted each of these great, natural grasslands into productive farmland and ranches have much in common. Fig. 23 summarises the sequence of occupation and expansion and the results at each stage.

IV The Effects of Morphogenic Processes

Under natural conditions a grass cover and organic mat slow down morphogenic processes. But in the drier parts of the grasslands, and where over-cultivation or grazing leaves unprotected surfaces, agents of erosion may be particularly active over short periods.

The temperate grasslands as a whole have drainage networks and stream courses. In spring, the effects of hard frost favour surface run-off, for melting snow provides much surface water over hard ground. In all the grasslands the contribution of groundwater to rivers is relatively small: in the steppes the surface run-off in spring is some 60–80 per cent of the rainfall/snow-melt total. This causes both sheet erosion and gulleying. Minor erosion channels also take the excess surface water during the torrential summer storms. On degraded grassland, concentrated run-off over short periods is apt to create a drainage network of vertical gullies.

In arable areas, soil exposure does not necessarily lead to a higher surface run-off. In the Ukraine, for example, during spring unploughed

Fig. 24 These wheatlands near Regina show contouring needed to prevent an extension of gulleying (top right) due to run-off towards the stream. Moist patches appear where melting ice blocks created depressions, typical features of the northern prairies (top left).

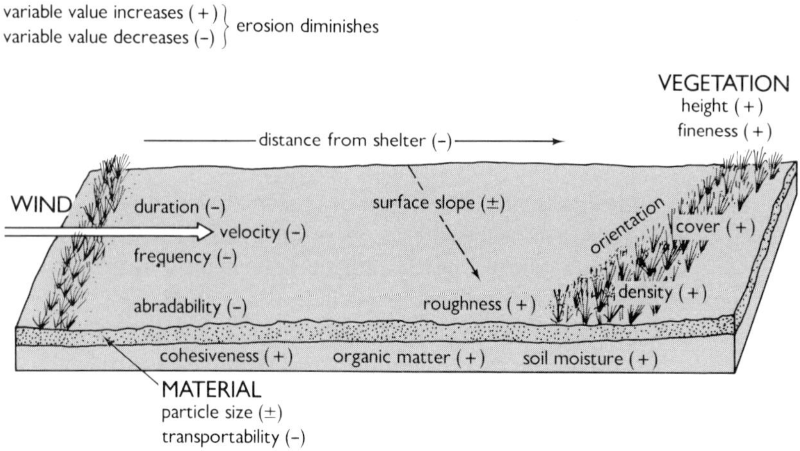

Fig. 25 The topography and open nature of the grasslands puts them at risk from wind erosion. The diagram shows interacting variables which diminish or increase the threat.

land with stubble was found to lose 71 per cent of the rainfall/snow-melt water as run-off, whereas adjacent newly-ploughed land shed only 6 per cent. Amid ranchland the nature of the grass-covering affects both the run-off and the sediment removed through the drainage system. A non-grazed basin in Colorado ranching country was found to have annual run-off some 30 per cent less than adjacent pasture land, with 45 per cent less sediment yield[12]. The mean annual suspended sediment concentration in streams tends to increase from humid grassland to dry grassland, to scrub country.

Wind has been responsible for mantling much of the prairies, steppes and pampas with loess; but the equilibrium of the grassland environment is usually delicately balanced, so that wind blowing across level landscapes also threatens erosion. Decomposing organic matter and secretory products of micro-organisms tend to bind the soil, especially when moist. But wind dries the surface and removes particles from loosely-bound material. Splash erosion by large drops during intense storms also loosens the surface, so that subsequent wash is able to transport the particles.

Surfaces left bare and loose through over-cultivation or over-grazing may deteriorate rapidly. The particles are lifted by the wind and moved forward in a flat trajectory—movement by saltation. Impacts by saltating particles can set other particles in motion, so that an avalanche effect causes more and more particles to be borne by the wind, with increasing surface abrasion. Surface roughness helps to reduce wind velocity; hence non-erodible material, such as stones, help to check erosion. The amount of non-erodible surface matter tends to increase as

Fig. 26 Wide tree belts are planted over thousands of kilometres of steppe. Like these near the Volga, they help to check wind erosion and may increase rainfall and dew formation.

wind removes the finer particles, and ultimately may shelter erodible material and thus create a wind-stable surface. Plants and plant residues also reduce near-surface wind velocity, as does rough ploughing.

Strip cropping restricts soil avalanching, and so does the practice of leaving stubble between strips of ploughed land, normal to the prevailing wind. The strips are wide enough to prevent saltating particles from jumping them; they trap the particles and also reduce the near-surface wind velocity.

The combined effects of rainfall variability and wind action are often seen in minor features on the grasslands. For example, the streams, which vary in volume, expose stretches of the bed to the wind, so that the leeward side of their valleys becomes blanketed by sand deposits. In places along the Arkansas and Missouri valleys dunes have developed on the leeward sides.

As the world's arable areas are being extended, soil carbon reserves created by grasslands continue to be depleted as oxidation releases carbon dioxide. This transfers almost as much carbon dioxide to the atmosphere each year as the burning of fossil fuels. Atmospheric carbon dioxide is responsible for 'a greenhouse effect' which warms the atmosphere, so that the continuing build-up should make the lower atmosphere hotter. Thus the conversion of more grassland to arable to feed future generations may not only lead to soil carbon depletion, but cause climatic changes, with a chain of physical and economic consequences.

Problems of Development—Four Cases

Wherever men have transformed the natural grasslands, they have made serious initial errors, largely through disturbing a delicately-balanced ecological stability. Even now many established farmers live precariously on these apparently productive lands. The following examples show that careful organisation and a high energy input are needed to make the most of these temperate grasslands.

Trial and Error—the High Veld

The development of South Africa's High Veld illustrates many of the problems resulting from rapid occupation and farming on a trial and error basis during the initial period. Here the 'red grass', a metre or so tall, covered the undulating landscape, 1000–2000 m above sea-level. Mean monthly temperatures range from 8–22°C, and evaporation rates are generally high. The annual rainfall is some 500–750 mm, but most falls in summer storms, so that grasses quickly lose nutrient value in the

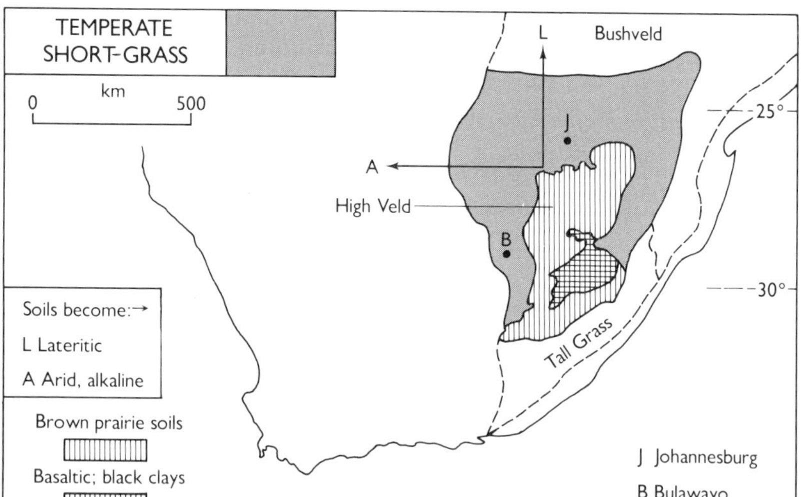

Fig. 27 The location of South Africa's High Veld, showing the main area of podsolic brown soils and those derived from old volcanic flows. Westwards the soils become drier, sandier and more saline; northwards they have ferruginous characteristics of shallow savanna soils. The grassland climates are modified by altitude.

dry winter. The organic content of the soils is lower than on the steppes and prairies, and many lack calcium, magnesium and potassium—although the black clays developed on volcanic rocks have proved excellent for maize-growing.

Merino sheep were established on the grasslands in the 19th century. But soon over-stocking and veld burning, to improve pastures just before the summer rains, led to serious erosion, with gulleying and dust bowl conditions. Maize-growing on the better land had developed into monoculture by the 1920s, causing soil deterioration and erosion by the 1930s. Soil erosion remains a major problem; but, more recently, the development of the Vaal river system for irrigation, changes to mixed farming, crop rotation with fodder plants, the use of fertilisers and much State assistance have produced high-yielding agricultural land—though, again, only through a great expenditure of energy. Nevertheless, a great deal of the High Veld remains as improved pasture for sheep and cattle.

Land Tenure Problems—the Pampas

The pattern of land-holdings on the Argentine pampas has long affected the land-use and productivity of these potentially rich lowlands[13]. Many of the landowners who acquired large estates in the 19th century were content with an income based on low yields from a large part of their

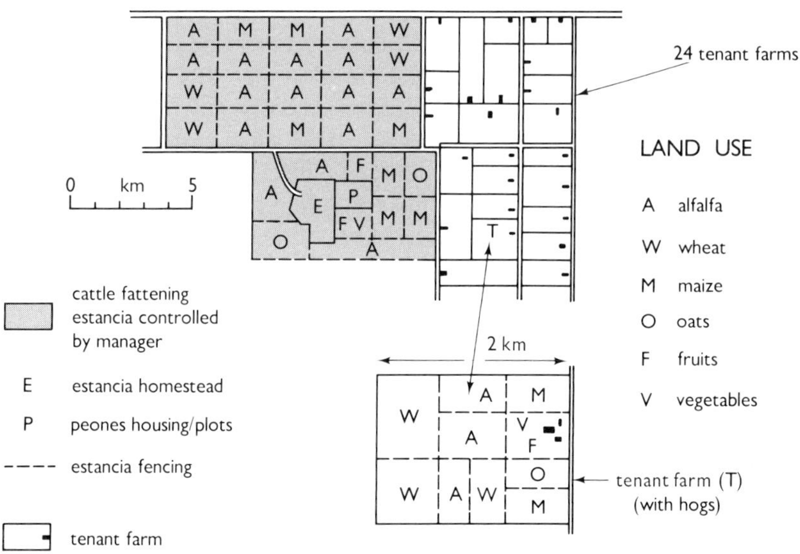

Fig. 28 Land-use on the pampas, based on an estancia of 15 000 hectares, a sub-division of a 19th-century land grant of 40 000 hectares in Buenos Aires province. 6 500 hectares are leased to 24 tenant farmers. The main estancia specialises in purchasing and fattening cattle.

estate, and sub-divided the rest into smaller tenant farms. In the early days an immigrant tenant family would hold the land for a short, agreed period, establish alfalfa to yield a fodder crop for five years, follow it with a wheat crop, and then move on. New tenants were then acquired to replant alfalfa. Since then, legal guarantees for longer, renewable tenancies and rights to purchase have perpetuated a mosaic of huge enclosures and many small holdings.

The big farms, supervised by a manager, retain a great deal of pasture and grow grain in large enclosures, with the help of hired resident workers. The family farms are usually more intensively cultivated, though many are not large enough for efficient mechanised agriculture and are under-capitalised. The same is true in those parts of the pampas where small holdings were created by colonisation schemes. Today they are often too small to provide a good living. In some places amalgamation has produced more efficient units. In others the large farms are being sub-divided into workable areas. But generally the agrarian structure has acted against the best use of one of the world's most fertile lowlands.

Adjusting the Land-use Pattern—the Canadian Prairies

The location of the main wheat areas has changed with the years in response to 'trial and error' settlement, the effects of climatic variations, changes in regional land values, technological improvements, and world demands[14].

High wheat prices after World War I encouraged the expansion of wheat-growing into marginal areas, as did the good years 1927 and 1928. Then came the 1930s droughts, which emphasised that many of the marginal lands were really unsuitable for wheat. Much of eastern Alberta has insufficient rain, inferior soils, and a high hail risk; south-west Saskatchewan has unreliable rainfall and suffered serious wind erosion. At the same time, the black soils of eastern Alberta appeared more profitable for livestock, and south-west Manitoba, despite its summer heat and moisture and high wheat yields, found that other crops were profitable, such as oilseeds; also its nearness to eastern markets favoured livestock. In all these areas there was a decrease in wheat-growing, but an increase on the black and brown soils of central Saskatchewan.

World War II disrupted grain production and favoured stock farming, but in the 1950s wheat-growing expanded to supply war-torn Europe. In the mid-sixties, after a period of over-production, enormous sales were made to USSR and China. The resulting expansion into marginal areas now had the advantages of hindsight and new technology. On vulnerable land, stubble was left to reduce wind erosion and trap snow, and sub-surface weed-cutters helped conserve moisture—so that a profitable

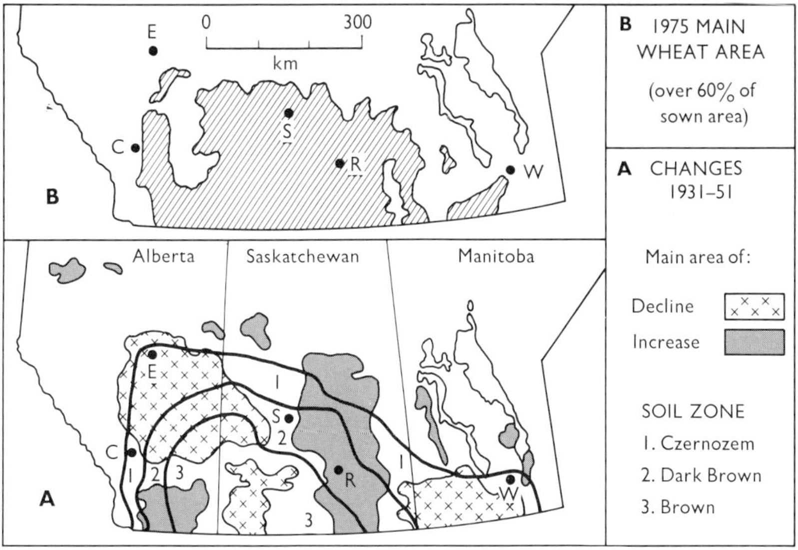

Fig. 29 A shows changes in the main wheat-growing areas of Canada's prairie provinces, and B the results of more recent expansion, which owes much to the use of new techniques and greater energy inputs. (• Regional cities)

wheat/wheat/fallow replaced wheat/fallow rotation. At the same time, weed killers, nitrate and phosphate fertilisers, solid-stem wheats (to withstand hollow-stem wheat pests) and the introduction of rust-resistant varieties produced higher yields from the main areas, where land values increased.

Fig. 30 Cattle cross river flats in south-western Alberta on their way to summer pastures. The farmers grow fodder to supplement winter feed.

Fig. 31 The many tree-sheltered homesteads reflect the fact that the climate and soils of these eastern prairies, in Manitoba, have favoured closer, mixed farming, though grain yields are high.

With high inputs farmers need high returns and stable demands, for switching from one enterprise to another is costly. Their vulnerability was demonstrated when the disasters in USSR's Virgin Lands in 1963 and 1965 led to huge demands for Canadian wheat, which declined abruptly when 1966 brought a record harvest to the steppes.

Wheat Harvest and Hazards—the Prairies

Some two hundred crews, each of 7–10 'custom cutters', bring in the wheat from Texas, in May, to the Canadian border, in September. Their activities highlight the difficulties and occasional disasters which still attend large-scale wheat-farming.

A crew takes with it perhaps four huge combines and trucks, pick-up vehicles, and house trailers. They work continuously in shifts, moving northwards from one farm to another on contract, and maintaining their machinery. In wheatfields of several hundred hectares, each combine moves at about 5 kph and cuts a 7 metre-wide path, in diminishing rectangles. Grain trucks shuttle between the combines and railside storage bins or elevators.

The report of a crew for one particular season[15] showed that in Texas

Fig. 32 (*Above*) wheat harvest on the level prairies in Kansas. (*Below*) irrigation for alfalfa on the dry western plains of Montana.

drought had so withered the hard, red winter wheat that, through low cutting, rocks damaged the harvesters; on some farms harvesting was impossible. Yet in Oklahoma rain delayed cutting, and in some counties hail had damaged a large proportion of the crop before harvest. Timing is important: farmers want quick cutting at the exact moment the grain is ready, to avoid loss through rain, hail or fire. In Kansas the farmers and cutters enjoyed a bumper harvest. In Colorado fire swept through a wheatfield destroying a truck. In Montana a skunk was 'harvested' and polluted a combine! In all, a vivid picture of mechanised activity over an enormous area—rural, and completely changed from the grasslands of a few generations ago—but maintained only by large inputs of energy and still suffering from climatic vagaries and their effects on soil structure.

Conservation of Genetic Material from the Grasslands

Grasses of the wild ancestral species have been largely replaced by highly-bred food plants. Yet it is vital that the former are preserved, for they may be introduced by back-breeding to enable food plants to cope with disease or drought. Hence the importance of establishing world reserves of genetic material and the creation of gene banks.

References

[1]T. R. OKE (1978) Boundary Layer Climates, Chap. 4 & 5 (Methuen)
[2]D. FARNEY (1980) The Tall Grass Prairie *Nat. Geographic* **157** p. 37
[3]H. WALTER (1972) Vegetation of the Earth, Chap. 7 p. 193 (Springer-Verlag)
[4]V. E. SHELFORD (1978) The Ecology of North America, Chap. 13 p. 328 (Univ. of Illinois)
[5]D. C. MONEY (1978) Climate, Soils and Vegetation, p. 175 (UTP)
[6]J. MADSON (1978) Nebraska's Sand Hills *Nat. Geographic* **154** p. 493
[7]J. G. NELSON (1975) Prairie Without Much Grass *Geog. Mag.* **47** p. 614
[8]N. PEARS (1977) Basic Biogeography, p. 81 (Longman)
[9]K. W. BUTZER (1979) This Is Indian Country *Geog. Mag.* **52** p. 140
[10]M. J. BOWDEN (1980) Creating Cowboy Country *Geog. Mag.* **52** p. 693
[11]J. H. PATERSON (1979) North America, Chap. 18 p. 319 (OUP)
[12]K. J. GREGORY, D. E. WALLING (1976) Drainage Basin Form and Process, p. 347 (Arnold)
[13]J. C. CROSSLEY (1971) The River Plate Countries: Latin American Geographical Perspectives (ed. H. BLAKEMORE, C. T. SMITH), p. 446 (Methuen)
[14]T. S. DUNLOP (1970) Changes in the Canadian Wheat Belt 1931–69 *Geography* **55** p. 157
[15]N. GROVE (1972) North with the Wheat Cutters *Nat. Geographic* **142** p. 194

Other Sources

J. C. DEWDNEY (1979) A Geography of the Soviet Union (Pergamon)
G. H. DURY (1979) Vast Continent with a Simple Layout *Geog. Mag.* **52** p. 37
S. R. EYRE (1975) Vegetation and Soils (Arnold)
P. ODUM (1975) Ecology (Holt-Saunders)
N. POLUNIN (1960) Introduction to Plant Geography (Longman)
G. RIKLER *et al.* (1976) The Soviet Land Revealed *Geog. Mag.* **48** p. 266
I. G. SIMMONS (1979) Biogeography: Natural and Cultural (Arnold)
J. TIVY (1979) Biogeography (Oliver & Boyd)

Points for Discussion

1 'Temperate Grasslands' as an adequate description of the parts of the world considered here.

2 Continentality and its influences on climates, vegetation and land-use.

3 Fundamental differences between the prairies, steppes and pampas.

4 The influences of past climatic conditions on present soil conditions and land-use.

5 The limitation of using mean monthly rainfall and temperature figures to show conditions on the grasslands; the kind of climatic information required.

6 The significance of micro-climatic data for grassland areas and how it may be used.

7 Why shrubs and trees occur in some parts of prairies and steppes, yet are generally absent.

8 The significance of the formation of a turf mat on the grasslands.

9 How surface materials are transported by agents of erosion. The circumstances under which these processes affect the plainlands.

10 The dangers of interfering with existing animal populations.

11 The reasons for man's large and increasing input of energy into the prairies, and the effects of this.

12 Definitions of 'extensive' and 'intensive' farming, and why the distinction between them becomes blurred.

13 The effects of increasing world population on the grasslands.

14 The effects of increasing mechanisation and larger farms on grassland populations and social geography.

15 The changing roles of forms of communication and transport in developing the grasslands.

16 Vegetation is used in a number of different ways in order to preserve soil fertility in arable areas.

17 Reorganisation of systems of land tenure has proved necessary in order to make efficient use of the grasslands.

18 The consequences of releasing soil carbon reserves to the atmosphere.

Glossary

air mass a large air body of considerable depth in which horizontal temperature and humidity gradients are relatively slight
albedo a measure of the ability of a surface to reflect insolation
alfalfa (lucerne) a perennial forage crop related to clovers whose root bacteria fix nitrogen from the air and enrich soils
aquifer rock which holds and permits the passage of water
axial bud one formed in the angle (axil) between stem and leaf
biomass the total plant and animal material in a given system (stated as dry weight)
biotic pertaining to life
calcareous containing calcium carbonate
carnivore animal which eats mainly flesh
Chinook wind maritime air dried by passage over the Rocky Mountains and warmed by compression on sinking
ecosystem a complex integrated system in which living communities and their non-living environment interact
evapo-transpiration the combined loss of water from surfaces and by transpiration from plants
forb herb of other than grass habit
friable soil one which is easy to crumble
gene a unit of material within a cell which influences a particular set of characteristics in the organism
geomorphic related to the shape of landforms
geophyte plant developing from underground bulb, tuber or rhizome
herbaceous vegetation of flowering plants whose stems are not woody
herbivore animal which mainly eats herbs
humus a substance produced by the slow decomposition and oxidation of organic matter on, or near, the surface
insolation energy radiated by the sun
ion an atom, or group of atoms, positively charged through losing electrons (cation) or negatively charged through gaining electrons (anion)
leaching removal of soil materials in solution by percolating water
legume plant of the order of Leguminosae, whose root nodules have nitrogen-fixing bacteria; they enrich the soil with nitrogenous compounds
lichen algae and fungus growing together for mutal advantage
lithosphere the solid outer crust of the earth
loess an unstratified deposit of fine wind-borne materials
nitrifying conversion of nitrogen or nitrogen compounds to substances which can be used in biological processes
nutrient provider of food
organic acid one derived from the decomposition of living matter (as opposed to the wider chemical definition)
pedalfer soil with accumulation of aluminium and iron compounds, poor in calcium carbonate
pedocal soil rich in calcium carbonate
pH value a measure of the degree of acidity or alkalinity of soil (neutral 7.0—acid smaller values, alkaline larger values)
photosynthesis the conversion of carbon dioxide and water into organic compounds by solar energy and plant chlorophyll
predator animal that seizes, and usually consumes, living prey
prismatic structure soil material aggregated into columns, like long prisms
protoplasm the fluid making up the cells of living organisms; it contains proteins
regolith a mantle of debris and material weathered from and covering the bedrock
rhizome horizontal underground stem which sends up shoots at intervals
rodent a gnawing mammal
saltation forward movement of a particle along a surface by a series of skips or jumps
sedges perennial grass-like herbs (family Cyperaceae)
share-cropper tenant receiving seed, fertiliser etc. from an owner who takes a share of the crop
Temperate lands lying between Tropical and Polar climatic zones (but those in continental interiors subject to climatic extremes)
tiller a lateral shoot from the axial bud at the base of a grass stem
xerophytic vegetation adapted to dry environmental conditions